Worry, Worry, Go Away!

A Kid's Book About Worry and Anxiety

Written by Christine A. Adams, M.A.

Illustrated by R.W. Alley

ABBEY PRESS

Abbey Press Publications
St. Meinrad, IN 47577

THIS BOOK IS DEDICATED
to my grandchildren:
Harrison Edward Hanley
Benjamin Michael Firsick
James Elliot Firsick
Grace Lenore Christine Hanley
Diana Mary Butch
Katie Butch

Text © 2012 Christine A. Adams, M.A.
Illustrations © 2012 Saint Meinrad Archabbey
Published by Abbey Press Publications
St. Meinrad, Indiana 47577

Library of Congress Catalog Number
2011940228

ISBN 978-0-87029-471-6

Printed in the United States of America.

A Message to Parents, Teachers, and Other Caring Adults

All kids experience normal worries—separation anxiety, stranger anxiety, fear of monsters in the dark, or of a circus clown—different circumstances, real and imagined. To overcome these anxieties, a child needs to understand what worry is, where it comes from, and how to challenge and contain it.

Since young children don't know that being afraid isn't the same as being in danger, they believe that their worries make sense. Unless they are given other guidance, they are often left listening to negative self-talk. For this reason, therapists use Cognitive Behavioral Therapy to help kids with anxiety.

Working through worry and anxiety is extremely important because many teen and adult anxiety disorders start in childhood. The presence, and the example, of a responsive and informed parent or helper can establish patterns of behavior and thinking that could last a lifetime.

With this "psycho-educational" approach, kids are taught to question the accuracy of their first reaction, which is: "What *if* the 'most awful thing' happens?" They learn to STOP, to THINK TWICE, and to identify "What else *might* happen?" They are taught to deal with the normal physical reactions of fear and anxiety through relaxation techniques and visualization.

Using this approach, they can reappraise what they fear with new thinking and calm breathing. Finally, when they are ready, they can overcome their fear with a step-by-step exposure to it.

Some children's worries are related to performance and general self-esteem issues. It's important to remind children of how special they are and how far they've come in overcoming previous fears.

Finally, kids need to know they're not alone, but have a supportive parent or adult to listen to them. They need to believe that when that parent or adult is not available, God is always there with them, beside them, all around them, surrounding them with His Love.

—Christine A. Adams, M.A., and Robert J. Butch, LICSW

What Is a Worry?

A worry is an idea that pops into your mind when you're scared. It may be real or "make believe."

You have a wonder-ful mind. It talks to you about real things and "make believe" things. It might say you are in real danger, or that someone won't like you, or will make fun of you. That is your "worry voice" saying, "What if something bad happens?"

Your "smart voice" tells you that these worries might not be true. Your "smart voice" says "What else could happen—maybe it won't be so bad?"

Remember, God gave you your wonder-ful mind. God helps you use your "smart voice" to figure out what's real and "make believe."

When We Need to Listen to Our Worry Voice

Grown-ups tell us to look both ways when we cross the street, not to talk to strangers, and not to play with matches. We need to listen when our "worry voice" tells us to stay safe.

When we "worry" about getting a bad grade, we do our homework and study our spelling words. It's good when we listen to our "worry voice" telling us to do our best.

Sometimes, though, the "worry voice" gets turned on and there's nothing to be afraid of, like with bugs, monsters, or thunderstorms—or it says we can't do something when we can. That's not so good.

Your job is to turn on your "smart voice." It will tell you to STOP and THINK TWICE, to breathe and relax, and figure out if you should listen or not.

Where Do Worries Come From?

Some movies, TV shows, and books can make us worry. It's easy to get mixed up about what's real and what's "make believe."

Everybody feels afraid sometimes; but when you're a kid, lots of things seem scary. You may hear and see things you don't understand. When you're afraid, talk to your parents or a helpful grown-up.

Talking about your worries makes you feel safer. It helps your fear fade away and stop your worries from growing.

When Worries Grow Into Anxiety

When you listen to the "worry voice" too much, your worries get bigger. They get louder in your mind and seem true, even when they're not. Somehow, worries get stuck and play over and over again. New ones pop up. This is called "anxiety."

Worry is like rain. A little bit is good. It makes plants grow, giving us food. But a lot of rain can be bad. It covers the ground so nothing can grow.

When you worry a little about a spelling test, you study and get a good grade. When you worry too much, you get anxious and forget the words.

Don't let anxiety take over and keep you from doing your best. Let God help you. Be a worry-wise kid!

Slow Down, Relax, and Breathe

When you feel fear, whether it's real or "make believe," you might begin sweating, have butterflies in your stomach, get a headache, and feel like you can't think straight.

When you feel nervous and jittery, turn on your "smart voice" and remind yourself to slow down. Take a deep breath—all the way into your belly. Hold that breath while you count slowly from 1 to 5. Let it out slowly and count from 1 to 5 again. Practice doing this now. If you do it 10 times, you'll be calm. No kidding.

Exercise is also very good for you. Your body calms down and worries slip away. Eat healthy foods, like plenty of fruits and veggies—and keep moving.

Talking Back to the Worry Voice

Your "smart voice" helps you talk back to your "worry voice." Say "STOP!" Push the stop button in your mind and ask questions. "What is really true?" "What might be true?" "Could I be worrying for nothing?"

Felipe was playing baseball and he was up at bat. His "worry voice" said, "What if you strike out?" His "smart voice" said "STOP" and Felipe said to himself, "I can see myself hitting a single right down the middle." In his mind he pictured it. Guess what happened…he hit the first pitch right down the middle!

Listen to your "smart voice." It's God helping you. Be a worry-wise kid!

When Your Worry Voice Keeps Bugging You

When your "worry voice" doesn't listen to you, hit the STOP button again and say, "Worry, worry go away. Don't come back today!" "Get lost, worry voice!"

Get busy playing a game, listening to music, watching TV, or reading a book. If the "worry voice" follows you around while you're playing, whispering worries in your ear, get tough and say "Get lost, worry voice!"

If it comes back, try this: in your mind, make up a small black box called a "worry box." Think of yourself taking your worries and stuffing them into that box. Then picture yourself giving your "worry box" to God.

Another trick is to close your eyes, take deep breaths, and think of being in a happy, safe place. It will take your mind off your worries.

You're the Boss of Your Thinking

You can flip the switch in your mind anytime you want to. Shaun wanted to do well in school. In third grade, he said, "I should get all A's in school. If I get a B, I'm a failure." Telling himself he could be a "failure" was not a good way to talk to himself.

Shaun flipped the switch and tuned into his "smart voice." He said to himself, "I should try to get all A's, but if I get a B, I will know I tried my best."

When *you* are your own best friend, you don't listen to the idea that says, "I can't do this because I'm not good enough." You flip the switch and tell yourself, "I can do this. I'm smart enough to try by myself and I'm smart enough to ask for help." When you always try to do your best, you're not a failure.

Face the Fear...Step by Step

Latisha was afraid to ride her bike. But she didn't listen to the "worry voice." She got on again and tried. She almost slipped off, but she put her foot down and balanced the bike. She kept trying and was soon riding with the wind in her face.

If you're shy, making friends can be hard. Start by making one friend at school, then one in your church, and then one in your neighborhood. Pretty soon, you'll be too busy to think about being shy.

When things change, or we start something new, we worry about what is next. Like when we change from first to second grade, or move to a new town. Remember, everything happens one step at a time. Use your "smart voice" to talk you through each step.

You can't run away from fear. When you don't run, but turn around and face the fear, it backs off. When you're ready, practice facing your fear—one step at a time.

Worries about Tomorrow, or Yesterday

Sometimes your "worry voice" talks about what might happen in the future. Like, "What will the teacher say if I forget my homework?" or "What if my dad loses his job?" Your "worry voice" is fooling you! It's giving you anxiety over something that's not true.

Sometimes your "worry voice" might go backwards to the past saying, "I am worried about Jake being mad at me because I didn't sit with him on the bus?" Your "worry voice" is fooling you again. Yesterday has already happened. Today, all you can do is ask Jake if he's upset and go sit with him.

Nobody knows exactly what will happen tomorrow, and yesterday is gone. Just remember, God always watches over you.

Find a Helpful Grown-Up

Talk about your worries to a helpful grown-up. As soon as you tell someone, you feel calmer. Your stomach ache may disappear, your heart will stop racing, and your headache will go away.

Sometimes when worries seem really big, your mom might suggest you talk to someone special like a counselor. That's a good thing.

Ask your parents, or a helpful adult, to make "alone" time with you. This is when you can take your worries out of your "worry box" and share them.

Ben was nervous right before he had to play the piano. His mom knew he needed some "alone" time, so she took him aside. He told her he was nervous about making a mistake. She reassured him by saying, "As long as you try, it's OK." Ben walked on the stage and said to himself, "It's not the end of the world. I'll do my best!" And he did.

You've Come a Long Way

When you were two, you worried when your mom left the room. Sometimes you cried and wouldn't let go of her. When you were four, you didn't even notice when she left.

When you were five, you were a little nervous about kindergarten, so your mom took you. Now, you can't wait for her to leave so you can see Katie and Ryan.

You don't face fears all at once; you do it a little bit at a time. If something in school makes you anxious, don't avoid it and stay home. You're growing and changing all the time—what bothers you today will be gone tomorrow.

Remember what you learned in this book. You are stronger than worries and don't have to listen to the "worry voice." Know that God gives you great strength.

You Are Special Just the Way You Are

You don't have to be the fastest, smartest, or best looking kid to feel good about yourself. Guess what? Don't listen to the "worry voice" that says you always have to be the best at everything.

No one is best at everything. Some kids do math but can't play baseball. Some kids play baseball but can't play the violin. Some kids play the violin but can't do math. You have your own special gift.

You don't need to do anything special to be special— you already are!

God Is Always with You

If you have to be away from your mom and dad for a while, God is there beside you. When you sing a solo with the chorus, God stands on the stage beside you. When you answer in class, God is there.

God always has time to listen to you. You can tell God if you're upset, worried, or scared. Praying and talking to God are the same thing. God will understand. He will help with your "smart voice."

Right beside you, deep inside you, God surrounds you with His love. You can do many wonderful, brave new things with God's help.

When you are scared, or worried, tell yourself, "I am a child of God. God is with me, right now."

Christine A. Adams, M.A., has spent 32 years teaching and counseling teens. She is the author of 12 books published in 21 countries (see www.christineaadams.com). Chris has three grown children and four grandchildren and lives in Maine with her husband, Robert J. Butch, LICSW, who co-authored *Happy to Be Me: A Kid's Book About Self-esteem.*

Robert J. Butch, LICSW, is a licensed clinical social worker who is certified in Maine, New Hampshire, and Massachusetts. Since he has worked with children with anxiety disorders and counseled with an emphasis on child and family issues, he contributed to *Worry, Worry, Go Away! A Kid's Book About Worry and Anxiety* as a professional consultant bringing his clinical expertise to the content.

R. W. Alley is the illustrator for the popular Abbey Press adult series of Elf-help books, as well as an illustrator and writer of children's books. He lives in Barrington, Rhode Island, with his wife, daughter, and son. See a wide variety of his works at: www.rwalley.com.